Japanese Cheesecake Cookbook
Indulge in the Fluffy and Irresistible World of Japanese Cheesecakes

JAPANESE CHEESECAKE COOKBOOK

First edition. February 1, 2024.

ISBN: 979-8224874538

Written by john ahmad.

Table of Contents

John Ahmad

Chapter 1: Introduction to Japanese Cheesecakes

Japanese cheesecakes, often referred to as "soufflé cheesecakes," are a culinary sensation that has taken the dessert world by storm. These delicate and airy confections boast a distinct texture and flavor profile that sets them apart from traditional cheesecakes. In this chapter, we embark on a journey into the captivating realm of Japanese cheesecakes, exploring their origins, unique characteristics, essential ingredients, and the art of crafting these ethereal treats.

Origins and Evolution: A Blend of Cultures

The story of Japanese cheesecakes is one of cultural fusion and culinary innovation. Dating back to the late 19th century during Japan's Meiji period, the nation experienced an influx of Western influences. Cheesecakes, a beloved Western dessert, found their way onto Japanese dessert menus, inspiring local pastry chefs to adapt and transform the recipe to suit Japanese tastes. Through experimentation and creativity, the Japanese cheesecake emerged as a delightful synthesis of East and West.

The Japanese Cheesecake Experience: Light as Air, Rich in Flavor

At the heart of the Japanese cheesecake's allure is its extraordinary texture – a harmonious balance between ethereal lightness and decadent creaminess. Achieving this texture requires a delicate interplay of ingredients and techniques. The result is a cake that seems to defy gravity, effortlessly melting in your mouth with each forkful.

Key Ingredients and Their Roles: Crafting Perfection

Understanding the role of each ingredient is essential to mastering the art of Japanese cheesecake:

Cream Cheese Elegance: Premium cream cheese lends a luscious, tangy depth to the cake's flavor while contributing to its velvety smoothness.

Eggstravagant Delicacy: Egg whites, meticulously whipped to stiff peaks, provide the cake's signature lightness, giving it a delicate, melt-in-the-mouth quality.

Sweet Symphony: A restrained sweetness allows other flavors to shine while ensuring a balanced dessert that isn't overly cloying.

Dairy Dance: Milk and sometimes heavy cream or yogurt enrich the batter, adding moisture and contributing to the cake's luxurious mouthfeel.

Mastering Techniques: Crafting the Perfect Japanese Cheesecake

Achieving the remarkable texture of a Japanese cheesecake demands finesse and precision:

Meticulous Mixing: The base of the cake is formed by blending cream cheese, egg yolks, sugar, and flavorings until the mixture is impeccably smooth.

Whipped White Wonders: Whipping egg whites to stiff peaks requires patience and skill, as these whites are then gently folded into the batter to create the cake's distinctive lightness.

Baking Brilliance: The water bath technique, where the cake pan is placed in a larger pan of hot water, ensures even baking and minimizes the risk of cracks.

A World of Variations: Flavorful Adventures

While the classic Japanese cheesecake is a masterpiece on its own, inventive variations add a captivating twist:

Matcha Magic: Infuse the cake with the vibrant, grassy notes of matcha green tea, adding a touch of elegance to your creation.

Black Sesame Sophistication: Elevate your cheesecake with the nutty richness of black sesame, a flavor beloved in Japanese cuisine.

Fruitful Fusion: Integrate seasonal fruits like strawberries or citrus for a burst of freshness that complements the cake's subtlety.

Savoring Your Creation: Presentation and Pairings

As you venture into the realm of Japanese cheesecakes, learn the art of presentation and pairing to elevate the experience:

Plating Poetry: Explore creative ways to present your cheesecake, from minimalist elegance to artistic extravagance.

Beverage Ballet: Discover the ideal beverages – such as delicate teas or crisp wines – that harmonize beautifully with the nuanced flavors of Japanese cheesecakes.

With the foundation of Japanese cheesecakes laid bare, you're now equipped to delve deeper into the world of these delightful confections. As you flip the page, anticipate an exploration of flavors, techniques, and inspirations that will guide you through the enchanting realm of Japanese cheesecake creation. Prepare to whisk, fold, and bake your way to a realm of dessert perfection that is both delectable and captivating. Your journey has only just begun, and the art of Japanese cheesecakes awaits your discovery.

Chapter 2: Essential Ingredients and Tools

Embark on your journey to become a Japanese cheesecake virtuoso by delving into the intricate world of essential ingredients and tools. With these building blocks at your disposal, you'll be well-equipped to craft ethereal cheesecakes that captivate the senses and delight the palate.

Core Ingredients: Crafting Flavor and Texture

Cream Cheese Elegance: Opt for premium, full-fat cream cheese to impart a velvety richness and tangy undertones that form the heart of Japanese cheesecakes. Its smooth consistency ensures a creamy texture that balances the delicate structure.

Eggs, the Lightness Architects: Both egg yolks and egg whites play crucial roles. Egg yolks contribute to the cake's structure and flavor profile, while the egg whites, when expertly whipped to stiff peaks, introduce the characteristic airy and light quality.

Sugar, the Balancing Act: Sugar's role extends beyond sweetness. It aids in achieving the cake's desired texture and contributes to the surface's appealing golden-brown hue during baking.

Milk and Dairy Harmony: Incorporate dairy ingredients like whole milk, heavy cream, or yogurt to infuse moisture and a luxurious creaminess. This ensemble ensures the cake melts in your mouth with each forkful.

Flavor Enhancers: Elevating Your Creation

Vanilla Essence, a Timeless Classic: A dash of pure vanilla extract adds depth and warmth to the flavor profile, enhancing the overall taste experience.

Citrus Zest, a Burst of Freshness: Grate citrus zest, such as lemon or orange, to introduce a vibrant burst of aroma and tang, balancing the richness of the cream cheese

Matcha Green Tea Powder, an Earthy Elegance: Introduce the unique flavor of matcha green tea, celebrated for its earthy notes and vibrant green hue, elevating the cake's sophistication.

Sesame Paste, a Nutty Indulgence: Experiment with black sesame paste or other nut-based pastes to add layers of complexity and a pleasing nuttiness to your creation.

Tools of the Trade: Ensuring Precision

Springform Pan, the Foundation: A springform pan with a removable base simplifies cake removal, ensuring the delicate structure remains intact.

Mixing Bowls, for Harmonious Blending: Assorted mixing bowls in various sizes facilitate efficient ingredient preparation and seamless mixing.

Whisk and Spatula Duo, for Seamless Mixing: A combination of a wire whisk and a rubber spatula enables thorough blending and gentle folding, maintaining the batter's integrity.

Hand or Stand Mixer, the Whipping Wizards: Leverage the power of a mixer to whip egg whites to stiff peaks and create a smooth, homogeneous batter.

Fine-Mesh Strainer, for Silky Smoothness: Strain cream cheese mixtures through a fine-mesh strainer to eliminate any lumps and ensure a silky, velvety texture.

Water Bath Setup, the Baking Secret: Employ a larger pan filled with water to create a gentle, even baking environment that minimizes cracks and ensures uniform texture.

Kitchen Thermometer, for Precision Baking: Monitor the internal temperature to prevent overcooking, preserving the cake's delicate structure.

Cooling Rack, for Gradual Cooling: A cooling rack promotes even cooling, preventing moisture buildup and ensuring a flawless finish.

Preparation and Organization: The Key to Success

Readiness and Organization: Prioritize readiness by gathering all ingredients and tools before starting, ensuring a seamless and efficient baking process.

Measurements Matter: Utilize precise measuring cups and spoons to maintain the delicate balance of flavors and textures, ensuring consistent results.

Room Temperature Ingredients: Allow cream cheese and eggs to reach room temperature, ensuring easy blending and a uniform batter consistency.

Patience and Attention: Japanese cheesecakes thrive on attention to detail. Meticulously follow each step, from ingredient incorporation to baking, for exceptional outcomes.

Armed with this comprehensive understanding of essential ingredients and tools, you're poised to embark on a creative and flavorful journey into the heart of Japanese cheesecake mastery. As we progress through the subsequent chapters, you'll unlock the secrets behind transforming these foundational components into exquisite creations that are bound to captivate the senses and leave a lasting impression.

Chapter 3: Classic Japanese Cheesecake

Indulge in the timeless allure of a Classic Japanese Cheesecake – a delicate creation that embodies the essence of Japanese culinary finesse. In this chapter, we will delve deep into the art of crafting the quintessential Japanese cheesecake, renowned for its ethereal texture and balanced flavors.

Ingredients:

- 250g cream cheese, softened
- 50g unsalted butter
- 100ml whole milk
- 6 large eggs, separated
- 1 teaspoon vanilla extract
- 120g granulated sugar
- 60g cake flour
- 20g cornstarch
- 1/4 teaspoon salt
- Confectioners' sugar (for dusting)

Instructions:

Preparation:

Preheat your oven to 325°F (160°C). Grease the bottom and sides of a 9-inch (23cm) round springform pan and line the bottom with parchment paper.

Cream Cheese Mixture:

- In a heatproof bowl, melt the cream cheese, butter, and milk together. Stir until smooth and well combined. Let the mixture cool slightly.

- Whisk in the egg yolks and vanilla extract until fully incorporated.

Dry Ingredients:

- Sift the cake flour, cornstarch, and salt together. Gradually fold the dry mixture into the cream cheese mixture until smooth. Set aside.

Whipped Egg Whites:

- In a separate clean bowl, use an electric mixer to whip the egg whites until foamy. Gradually add the granulated sugar while continuing to whip.

- Whip the egg whites to stiff peaks, ensuring the meringue is glossy and holds its shape when the beaters are lifted.

Folding and Batter Assembly:

- Gently fold one-third of the whipped egg whites into the cream cheese mixture to lighten it.

- Carefully fold in the remaining egg whites in two batches until no streaks remain, maintaining the batter's airy consistency.

Baking:

- Pour the batter into the prepared springform pan. Tap the pan gently on the counter to release any large air bubbles.

- Place the springform pan into a larger baking pan. Create a water bath by adding hot water to the larger pan until it reaches about halfway up the sides of the springform pan.

- Bake in the preheated oven for approximately 1 hour and 10 minutes, or until the top is golden brown and the cake is set with a slight jiggle in the center.

Cooling:

- Once baked, turn off the oven and leave the cake inside for about 10 minutes with the oven door slightly ajar. This gradual cooling helps prevent cracks.

- Remove the cake from the oven and water bath. Run a knife around the edges of the cake to loosen it from the pan. Allow the cake to cool completely in the pan on a wire rack.

Finishing Touches:

- Once completely cooled, carefully remove the sides of the springform pan. Dust the top of the cake with a light layer of confectioners' sugar.

Serving:

- Slice the Classic Japanese Cheesecake with a sharp, clean knife. Serve each slice with a sense of wonder, appreciating the cloud-like texture and delicate flavor.

As you savor each bite of this Classic Japanese Cheesecake, relish in the harmony of flavors and the exquisitely light texture that makes Japanese cheesecakes a beloved culinary treasure. This timeless recipe serves as the foundation for your journey into the realm of Japanese cheesecake creation, preparing you for the adventures and variations that lie ahead.

Chapter 4: Matcha Green Tea Cheesecake

Embark on a journey to infuse the captivating essence of matcha green tea into the delicate world of Japanese cheesecakes. In this chapter, we'll explore how to craft a Matcha Green Tea Cheesecake – a harmonious blend of flavors that marries the earthy allure of matcha with the ethereal lightness of Japanese cheesecake.

Ingredients:

- 250g cream cheese, softened
- 50g unsalted butter
- 100ml whole milk
- 6 large eggs, separated
- 1 teaspoon vanilla extract
- 120g granulated sugar
- 60g cake flour
- 20g cornstarch
- 1/4 teaspoon salt
- 2 tablespoons high-quality matcha green tea powder
- Confectioners' sugar (for dusting)

Instructions:

Preparation:

- Preheat your oven to 325°F (160°C). Grease the bottom and sides of a 9-inch (23cm) round springform pan and line the bottom with parchment paper.

Cream Cheese Mixture:

- Melt the cream cheese, butter, and milk in a heatproof bowl.

Stir until smooth, then let the mixture cool slightly.

- Whisk in the egg yolks and vanilla extract until well combined.

Dry Ingredients with Matcha Infusion:

- Sift the cake flour, cornstarch, and matcha green tea powder together. Gradually fold the dry mixture into the cream cheese mixture until smooth. Set aside.

Whipped Egg Whites:

- In a clean bowl, use an electric mixer to whip the egg whites until foamy. Gradually add the granulated sugar while continuing to whip.

- Whip the egg whites to stiff peaks, achieving a glossy meringue that holds its shape.

Folding and Batter Assembly:

- Gently fold one-third of the whipped egg whites into the cream cheese mixture to lighten it.

- Carefully fold in the remaining egg whites in two batches, ensuring the batter maintains its airy consistency.

Baking:

- Pour the batter into the prepared springform pan. Tap the pan gently on the counter to release any large air bubbles.

- Place the springform pan into a larger baking pan. Create a water bath by adding hot water to the larger pan until it reaches about halfway up the sides of the springform pan.

- Bake in the preheated oven for approximately 1 hour and 10 minutes, or until the top is golden brown and the cake is set with a slight jiggle in the center.

Cooling and Unmolding:

- Turn off the oven and leave the cake inside for about 10 minutes with the oven door slightly ajar. This gradual cooling helps prevent cracks.

- Remove the cake from the oven and water bath. Run a knife around the edges of the cake to loosen it from the pan. Allow the cake to cool completely in the pan on a wire rack.

Finishing Touches:

- Once fully cooled, carefully remove the sides of the springform pan. Dust the top of the cake with a delicate layer of confectioners' sugar.

Serving and Savoring:

- With reverence for the flavors of matcha and the delicate texture of Japanese cheesecakes, slice the Matcha Green Tea Cheesecake. Each bite offers a sublime symphony of taste and texture that captures the essence of Japan's rich culinary heritage.

The Matcha Green Tea Cheesecake invites you to revel in the tranquil charm of matcha while embracing the artistry of Japanese cheesecake crafting. As you savor each slice, let the distinctive flavors and harmonious marriage of elements transport you to a realm of culinary wonder. Your exploration of Japanese cheesecake continues with this captivating rendition, setting the stage for further creative endeavors and delightful variations.

Chapter 5: Sakura Cherry Blossom Cheesecake

Step into the ephemeral beauty of spring with a Sakura Cherry Blossom Cheesecake – a delicate creation that captures the essence of Japan's iconic cherry blossoms. In this chapter, we'll embark on a culinary journey that infuses the subtle charm of cherry blossoms into the exquisite canvas of Japanese cheesecakes.

Ingredients:

- 250g cream cheese, softened
- 50g unsalted butter
- 100ml whole milk
- 6 large eggs, separated
- 1 teaspoon vanilla extract
- 120g granulated sugar
- 60g cake flour
- 20g cornstarch
- 1/4 teaspoon salt
- 1 teaspoon sakura cherry blossom extract (or cherry blossom syrup)
- Pink food coloring (optional)
- Confectioners' sugar (for dusting)

Instructions:

Preparation:

- Preheat your oven to 325°F (160°C). Grease the bottom and sides of a 9-inch (23cm) round springform pan and line the bottom with parchment paper.

Cream Cheese Mixture:

- Melt the cream cheese, butter, and milk in a heatproof bowl. Stir until smooth and allow the mixture to cool slightly.

- Whisk in the egg yolks and vanilla extract until fully combined.

Dry Ingredients with Sakura Infusion:

- Sift the cake flour, cornstarch, and salt together. Gradually fold the dry mixture into the cream cheese mixture until smooth.

- Add the sakura cherry blossom extract (or syrup) to infuse delicate floral notes. If desired, add a few drops of pink food coloring for a subtle hue.

Whipped Egg Whites:

- In a clean bowl, use an electric mixer to whip the egg whites until foamy. Gradually add the granulated sugar while continuing to whip.

- Whip the egg whites to stiff peaks, achieving a glossy meringue that holds its shape.

Folding and Batter Assembly:

- Gently fold one-third of the whipped egg whites into the cream cheese mixture to lighten it.

- Carefully fold in the remaining egg whites in two batches, ensuring the batter maintains its airy consistency.

Baking:

- Pour the batter into the prepared springform pan. Tap the pan gently on the counter to release any large air bubbles.

- Place the springform pan into a larger baking pan. Create a water bath by adding hot water to the larger pan until it reaches about halfway up the sides of the springform pan.

- Bake in the preheated oven for approximately 1 hour and 10 minutes, or until the top is golden brown and the cake is set with a slight jiggle in the center.

Cooling and Unmolding:

- Turn off the oven and leave the cake inside for about 10 minutes with the oven door slightly ajar. This gradual cooling helps prevent cracks.

- Remove the cake from the oven and water bath. Run a knife around the edges of the cake to loosen it from the pan. Allow the cake to cool completely in the pan on a wire rack.

Finishing Touches:

- Once fully cooled, carefully remove the sides of the springform pan. Dust the top of the cake with a delicate layer of confectioners' sugar.

Serving and Enchantment:

- As you slice the Sakura Cherry Blossom Cheesecake, you're invited to savor the delicate floral essence and enchanting flavor profile. Each bite transports you to the heart of springtime in Japan, celebrating the ephemeral beauty of cherry blossoms.

Chapter 6: Black Sesame Delight Cheesecake

Embark on a voyage to discover the rich and nutty flavors of black sesame with a Black Sesame Delight Cheesecake. In this chapter, we'll explore how to create a Japanese cheesecake that celebrates the elegance of black sesame while retaining the signature ethereal texture.

Ingredients:

- 250g cream cheese, softened
- 50g unsalted butter
- 100ml whole milk
- 6 large eggs, separated
- 1 teaspoon vanilla extract
- 120g granulated sugar
- 60g cake flour
- 20g cornstarch
- 1/4 teaspoon salt
- 3 tablespoons black sesame paste
- Confectioners' sugar (for dusting)

Instructions:

Preparation:

- Preheat your oven to 325°F (160°C). Grease the bottom and sides of a 9-inch (23cm) round springform pan and line the bottom with parchment paper.

Cream Cheese Mixture:

- Melt the cream cheese, butter, and milk in a heatproof bowl. Stir until smooth and allow the mixture to cool slightly.

- Whisk in the egg yolks and vanilla extract until fully combined.

Dry Ingredients with Black Sesame Infusion:

- Sift the cake flour, cornstarch, and salt together. Gradually fold the dry mixture into the cream cheese mixture until smooth.

- Incorporate the black sesame paste to infuse the batter with its distinctive nutty flavor.

Whipped Egg Whites:

- In a clean bowl, use an electric mixer to whip the egg whites until foamy. Gradually add the granulated sugar while continuing to whip.

- Whip the egg whites to stiff peaks, achieving a glossy meringue that holds its shape.

Folding and Batter Assembly:

- Gently fold one-third of the whipped egg whites into the cream cheese mixture to lighten it.

- Carefully fold in the remaining egg whites in two batches, ensuring the batter maintains its airy consistency.

Baking:

- Pour the batter into the prepared springform pan. Tap the pan gently on the counter to release any large air bubbles.

- Place the springform pan into a larger baking pan. Create a water bath by adding hot water to the larger pan until it reaches about halfway up the sides of the springform pan.

- Bake in the preheated oven for approximately 1 hour and 10 minutes, or until the top is golden brown and the cake is set with a slight jiggle in the center.

Cooling and Unmolding:

- Turn off the oven and leave the cake inside for about 10 minutes with the oven door slightly ajar. This gradual cooling helps prevent cracks.

- Remove the cake from the oven and water bath. Run a knife around the edges of the cake to loosen it from the pan. Allow the cake to cool completely in the pan on a wire rack.

Finishing Touches:

- Once fully cooled, carefully remove the sides of the springform pan. Dust the top of the cake with a delicate layer of confectioners' sugar.

Serving and Nutty Indulgence:

- As you indulge in each slice of the Black Sesame Delight Cheesecake, relish in the enchanting blend of flavors that black sesame brings. The nutty richness complements the airy texture, creating a symphony of taste and sensation.

Chapter 7: Yuzu Citrus Infusion Cheesecake

Embark on a zesty adventure with a Yuzu Citrus Infusion Cheesecake, where the bright and aromatic notes of yuzu elevate the art of Japanese cheesecakes. In this chapter, we'll explore how to create a cheesecake that harmoniously blends the refreshing essence of yuzu with the signature ethereal texture.

Ingredients:

- 250g cream cheese, softened
- 50g unsalted butter
- 100ml whole milk
- 6 large eggs, separated
- 1 teaspoon vanilla extract
- 120g granulated sugar
- 60g cake flour
- 20g cornstarch
- 1/4 teaspoon salt
- Zest and juice of 2 yuzu fruits (or 1 lemon and 1 lime)
- Confectioners' sugar (for dusting)

Instructions:

Preparation:

- Preheat your oven to 325°F (160°C). Grease the bottom and sides of a 9-inch (23cm) round springform pan and line the bottom with parchment paper.

Cream Cheese Mixture:

- Melt the cream cheese, butter, and milk in a heatproof bowl. Stir until smooth and allow the mixture to cool slightly.

- Whisk in the egg yolks and vanilla extract until fully combined.

Dry Ingredients with Citrus Zest and Yuzu Juice:

- Sift the cake flour, cornstarch, and salt together. Gradually fold the dry mixture into the cream cheese mixture until smooth.

- Add the zest and juice of the yuzu fruits (or lemon and lime) to infuse the batter with the bright and invigorating flavors.

Whipped Egg Whites:

- In a clean bowl, use an electric mixer to whip the egg whites until foamy. Gradually add the granulated sugar while continuing to whip.

- Whip the egg whites to stiff peaks, achieving a glossy meringue that holds its shape.

Folding and Batter Assembly:

- Gently fold one-third of the whipped egg whites into the cream cheese mixture to lighten it.

- Carefully fold in the remaining egg whites in two batches, ensuring the batter maintains its airy consistency.

Baking:

- Pour the batter into the prepared springform pan. Tap the pan gently on the counter to release any large air bubbles.

- Place the springform pan into a larger baking pan. Create a water bath by adding hot water to the larger pan until it reaches about halfway up the sides of the springform pan.

- Bake in the preheated oven for approximately 1 hour and 10 minutes, or until the top is golden brown and the cake is set with a slight jiggle in the center.

Cooling and Unmolding:

- Turn off the oven and leave the cake inside for about 10 minutes with the oven door slightly ajar. This gradual cooling helps prevent cracks.

- Remove the cake from the oven and water bath. Run a knife around the edges of the cake to loosen it from the pan. Allow the cake to cool completely in the pan on a wire rack.

Finishing Touches:

- Once fully cooled, carefully remove the sides of the springform pan. Dust the top of the cake with a delicate layer of confectioners' sugar.

Serving and Citrus Elegance:

As you relish each slice of the Yuzu Citrus Infusion Cheesecake, savor the invigorating and uplifting notes that yuzu brings. The citrus infusion adds a refreshing dimension to the exquisite texture, creating a symphony of flavor and sensation.

With the Yuzu Citrus Infusion Cheesecake, you're embarking on a journey that celebrates the vibrancy of yuzu while honoring the delicate craftsmanship of Japanese cheesecakes. Let each bite envelop you in the rejuvenating essence of citrus, guiding you toward the captivating variations and inspirations that await your exploration.

Chapter 8: Mochi and Red Bean Swirl Cheesecake

Embark on a fusion of textures and flavors with a Mochi and Red Bean Swirl Cheesecake, where the chewy delight of mochi and the earthy sweetness of red bean meet the ethereal elegance of Japanese cheesecakes. In this chapter, we'll explore how to craft a cheesecake that harmoniously blends these cherished elements into a captivating culinary masterpiece.

Ingredients:

- 250g cream cheese, softened
- 50g unsalted butter
- 100ml whole milk
- 6 large eggs, separated
- 1 teaspoon vanilla extract
- 120g granulated sugar
- 60g cake flour
- 20g cornstarch
- 1/4 teaspoon salt
- 1/2 cup sweetened red bean paste (anko)
- 1/2 cup cooked and mashed sweet mochi rice cakes
- Confectioners' sugar (for dusting)

Instructions:

Preparation:

- Preheat your oven to 325°F (160°C). Grease the bottom and sides of a 9-inch (23cm) round springform pan and line the bottom with parchment paper.

Cream Cheese Mixture:

- Melt the cream cheese, butter, and milk in a heatproof bowl. Stir until smooth and allow the mixture to cool slightly.

- Whisk in the egg yolks and vanilla extract until fully combined.

Dry Ingredients with Mochi and Red Bean Infusion:

- Sift the cake flour, cornstarch, and salt together. Gradually fold the dry mixture into the cream cheese mixture until smooth.

- Incorporate the mashed sweet mochi rice cakes, ensuring they are evenly distributed throughout the batter.

- Gently swirl in the sweetened red bean paste (anko) to create beautiful marbling effects.

Whipped Egg Whites:

- In a clean bowl, use an electric mixer to whip the egg whites until foamy. Gradually add the granulated sugar while continuing to whip.

- Whip the egg whites to stiff peaks, achieving a glossy meringue that holds its shape.

Folding and Batter Assembly:

- Gently fold one-third of the whipped egg whites into the cream cheese mixture to lighten it.

- Carefully fold in the remaining egg whites in two batches, ensuring the batter maintains its airy consistency.

Baking:

- Pour the batter into the prepared springform pan. Tap the pan gently on the counter to release any large air bubbles.

- Place the springform pan into a larger baking pan. Create a water bath by adding hot water to the larger pan until it reaches about halfway up the sides of the springform pan.

- Bake in the preheated oven for approximately 1 hour and 10 minutes, or until the top is golden brown and the cake is set with a slight jiggle in the center.

Cooling and Unmolding:

- Turn off the oven and leave the cake inside for about 10 minutes with the oven door slightly ajar. This gradual cooling helps prevent cracks.

- Remove the cake from the oven and water bath. Run a knife around the edges of the cake to loosen it from the pan. Allow the cake to cool completely in the pan on a wire rack.

Finishing Touches:

- Once fully cooled, carefully remove the sides of the springform pan. Dust the top of the cake with a delicate layer of confectioners' sugar.

Serving and Mochi Magic:

- With each slice of the Mochi and Red Bean Swirl Cheesecake, experience the delightful combination of creamy cheesecake, chewy mochi, and the comforting sweetness of red bean. The swirls of mochi and red bean create a visual and sensory masterpiece.

With the Mochi and Red Bean Swirl Cheesecake, you're embarking on a culinary journey that marries the enchantment of mochi and red bean with the intricate craftsmanship of Japanese cheesecakes. Allow each bite to transport you to a realm of unique flavors and textures, guiding you toward the intriguing variations and inspirations that beckon your exploration.

Chapter 9: Tropical Mango and Passionfruit Cheesecake

Embark on a journey to the tropics with a Tropical Mango and Passionfruit Cheesecake, where the luscious sweetness of mango and the tangy allure of passionfruit converge to create a tantalizing fusion. In this chapter, we'll explore how to craft a cheesecake that transports your taste buds to sun-kissed shores while retaining the delicate artistry of Japanese cheesecakes.

Ingredients:

- 250g cream cheese, softened
- 50g unsalted butter
- 100ml whole milk
- 6 large eggs, separated
- 1 teaspoon vanilla extract
- 120g granulated sugar
- 60g cake flour
- 20g cornstarch
- 1/4 teaspoon salt
- 1 ripe mango, pureed
- Pulp of 4 passionfruits (or passionfruit juice)
- Confectioners' sugar (for dusting)

Instructions:

Preparation:

- Preheat your oven to 325°F (160°C). Grease the bottom and sides of a 9-inch (23cm) round springform pan and line the bottom with parchment paper.

Cream Cheese Mixture:

- Melt the cream cheese, butter, and milk in a heatproof bowl. Stir until smooth and allow the mixture to cool slightly.

- Whisk in the egg yolks and vanilla extract until fully combined.

Dry Ingredients with Tropical Fruit Infusion:

- Sift the cake flour, cornstarch, and salt together. Gradually fold the dry mixture into the cream cheese mixture until smooth.

- Incorporate the pureed ripe mango, infusing the batter with the tropical sweetness of the fruit.

- Gently fold in the pulp of the passionfruits (or passionfruit juice) to add a tangy and exotic twist.

Whipped Egg Whites:

- In a clean bowl, use an electric mixer to whip the egg whites until foamy. Gradually add the granulated sugar while continuing to whip.

- Whip the egg whites to stiff peaks, achieving a glossy meringue that holds its shape.

Folding and Batter Assembly:

- Gently fold one-third of the whipped egg whites into the cream cheese mixture to lighten it.

- Carefully fold in the remaining egg whites in two batches, ensuring the batter maintains its airy consistency.

Baking:

- Pour the batter into the prepared springform pan. Tap the pan gently on the counter to release any large air bubbles.

- Place the springform pan into a larger baking pan. Create a water bath by adding hot water to the larger pan until it reaches about halfway up the sides of the springform pan.

- Bake in the preheated oven for approximately 1 hour and 10 minutes, or until the top is golden brown and the cake is set with a slight jiggle in the center.

Cooling and Unmolding:

- Turn off the oven and leave the cake inside for about 10 minutes with the oven door slightly ajar. This gradual cooling helps prevent cracks.

- Remove the cake from the oven and water bath. Run a knife around the edges of the cake to loosen it from the pan. Allow the cake to cool completely in the pan on a wire rack.

Finishing Touches:

- Once fully cooled, carefully remove the sides of the springform pan. Dust the top of the cake with a delicate layer of confectioners' sugar.

Serving and Tropical Bliss:

- As you relish each slice of the Tropical Mango and Passionfruit Cheesecake, experience the vibrant medley of flavors that mango and passionfruit bring. The tropical infusion adds a burst of sunshine to the heavenly texture, creating a symphony of taste and sensation.

Chapter 10: Decadent Chocolate Ganache Cheesecake

Indulge in the world of rich, velvety chocolate with a Decadent Chocolate Ganache Cheesecake, where the luxurious flavors of chocolate ganache meld with the ethereal lightness of Japanese cheesecake. In this chapter, we'll explore the art of crafting a cheesecake that marries the opulence of chocolate with the delicate finesse of Japanese culinary mastery.

Ingredients:

- 250g cream cheese, softened
- 50g unsalted butter
- 100ml whole milk
- 6 large eggs, separated
- 1 teaspoon vanilla extract
- 120g granulated sugar
- 60g cake flour
- 20g cornstarch
- 1/4 teaspoon salt
- 150g dark chocolate, melted and cooled
- Chocolate ganache (for topping)
- Cocoa powder (for dusting)

Instructions:

Preparation:

- Preheat your oven to 325°F (160°C). Grease the bottom and sides of a 9-inch (23cm) round springform pan and line the bottom with parchment paper.

Cream Cheese Mixture:

- Melt the cream cheese, butter, and milk in a heatproof bowl. Stir until smooth and allow the mixture to cool slightly.

- Whisk in the egg yolks and vanilla extract until fully combined.

Dry Ingredients with Chocolate Indulgence:

- Sift the cake flour, cornstarch, and salt together. Gradually fold the dry mixture into the cream cheese mixture until smooth.

- Add the melted and cooled dark chocolate, infusing the batter with the rich, decadent flavor.

Whipped Egg Whites:

- In a clean bowl, use an electric mixer to whip the egg whites until foamy. Gradually add the granulated sugar while continuing to whip.

- Whip the egg whites to stiff peaks, achieving a glossy meringue that holds its shape.

Folding and Batter Assembly:

- Gently fold one-third of the whipped egg whites into the cream cheese mixture to lighten it.

- Carefully fold in the remaining egg whites in two batches, ensuring the batter maintains its airy consistency.

Baking:

- Pour the batter into the prepared springform pan. Tap the pan gently on the counter to release any large air bubbles.

- Place the springform pan into a larger baking pan. Create a water bath by adding hot water to the larger pan until it reaches about halfway up the sides of the springform pan.

- Bake in the preheated oven for approximately 1 hour and 10 minutes, or until the top is golden brown and the cake is set with a slight jiggle in the center.

Cooling and Unmolding:

- Turn off the oven and leave the cake inside for about 10 minutes with the oven door slightly ajar. This gradual cooling helps prevent cracks.

- Remove the cake from the oven and water bath. Run a knife around the edges of the cake to loosen it from the pan. Allow the cake to cool completely in the pan on a wire rack.

Chocolate Ganache and Finishing Touches:

- Once fully cooled, spread a generous layer of chocolate ganache over the top of the cheesecake, allowing it to cascade down the sides.

- Dust the top of the ganache with a light layer of cocoa powder for an added touch of decadence.

Serving and Chocolate Bliss:

- As you savor each slice of the Decadent Chocolate Ganache Cheesecake, let the opulent chocolate flavors envelop your senses. The marriage of chocolate ganache and airy cheesecake creates a symphony of indulgence.

Chapter 11: Earl Grey Tea and Lavender Cheesecake

Embark on a journey of aromatic elegance with an Earl Grey Tea and Lavender Cheesecake, where the refined notes of Earl Grey tea and the soothing fragrance of lavender unite within the delicate canvas of Japanese cheesecake. In this chapter, we'll explore the art of crafting a cheesecake that encapsulates the harmonious symphony of floral and tea-infused flavors.

Ingredients:

- 250g cream cheese, softened
- 50g unsalted butter
- 100ml whole milk
- 6 large eggs, separated
- 1 teaspoon vanilla extract
- 120g granulated sugar
- 60g cake flour
- 20g cornstarch
- 1/4 teaspoon salt
- 2 Earl Grey tea bags (or loose tea leaves)
- 2 tablespoons culinary lavender buds
- Lavender-infused syrup (optional, for drizzling)
- Edible dried lavender flowers (for garnish)

Instructions:

Preparation:

- Preheat your oven to 325°F (160°C). Grease the bottom and sides of a 9-inch (23cm) round springform pan and line the bottom with parchment paper.

Cream Cheese Mixture:

- Melt the cream cheese, butter, and milk in a heatproof bowl. Stir until smooth and allow the mixture to cool slightly.

- Whisk in the egg yolks and vanilla extract until fully combined.

Dry Ingredients with Floral and Tea Infusion:

- Sift the cake flour, cornstarch, and salt together. Gradually fold the dry mixture into the cream cheese mixture until smooth.

- Brew the Earl Grey tea in hot water and allow it to cool. Add the brewed tea to the batter, infusing it with the delicate aroma of bergamot.

Whipped Egg Whites:

- In a clean bowl, use an electric mixer to whip the egg whites until foamy. Gradually add the granulated sugar while continuing to whip.

- Whip the egg whites to stiff peaks, achieving a glossy meringue that holds its shape.

Folding and Batter Assembly:

- Gently fold one-third of the whipped egg whites into the cream cheese mixture to lighten it.

- Carefully fold in the remaining egg whites in two batches, ensuring the batter maintains its airy consistency.

Baking:

- Pour the batter into the prepared springform pan. Tap the pan gently on the counter to release any large air bubbles.

- Place the springform pan into a larger baking pan. Create a water bath by adding hot water to the larger pan until it reaches about halfway up the sides of the springform pan.

- Bake in the preheated oven for approximately 1 hour and 10 minutes, or until the top is golden brown and the cake is set with a slight jiggle in the center.

Cooling and Unmolding:

- Turn off the oven and leave the cake inside for about 10 minutes with the oven door slightly ajar. This gradual cooling helps prevent cracks.

- Remove the cake from the oven and water bath. Run a knife around the edges of the cake to loosen it from the pan. Allow the cake to cool completely in the pan on a wire rack.

Lavender and Syrup Drizzle:

- While the cheesecake is cooling, crush the culinary lavender buds to release their fragrance. Sprinkle a light layer of crushed lavender over the top of the cake.

- Optionally, drizzle a lavender-infused syrup over the cake for an extra touch of floral sweetness.

Serving and Floral Elegance:

As you savor each slice of the Earl Grey Tea and Lavender Cheesecake, let the delicate interplay of tea and lavender unfold on your palate. The infusion of Earl Grey tea and lavender creates a captivating symphony of flavors.

Chapter 12: Japanese Cotton Cheesecake

Embark on a journey of cloud-like delight with a Japanese Cotton Cheesecake, where the ethereal texture of cotton-soft cheesecake takes center stage. In this chapter, we'll delve into the intricacies of creating a cheesecake that achieves the iconic lightness and delicate sweetness that Japanese cotton cheesecakes are renowned for.

Ingredients:

- 250g cream cheese, softened
- 50g unsalted butter
- 100ml whole milk
- 6 large eggs, separated
- 1 teaspoon vanilla extract
- 120g granulated sugar
- 60g cake flour
- 20g cornstarch
- 1/4 teaspoon salt
- 1/4 teaspoon cream of tartar
- Confectioners' sugar (for dusting)

Instructions:

Preparation:

- Preheat your oven to 325°F (160°C). Grease the bottom and sides of a 9-inch (23cm) round springform pan and line the bottom with parchment paper.

Cream Cheese Mixture:

- Melt the cream cheese, butter, and milk in a heatproof bowl.

Stir until smooth and allow the mixture to cool slightly.

- Whisk in the egg yolks and vanilla extract until fully combined.

Dry Ingredients for the Cotton Texture:

- Sift the cake flour, cornstarch, and salt together. Gradually fold the dry mixture into the cream cheese mixture until smooth.

Whipped Egg Whites and Cream of Tartar:

- In a clean, dry bowl, add the egg whites and cream of tartar.

- Use an electric mixer to whip the egg whites until they become foamy and slightly increase in volume.

- Gradually add the granulated sugar while continuing to whip.

- Whip the egg whites to soft peaks – they should be glossy and hold their shape.

Folding and Batter Assembly:

- Gently fold one-third of the whipped egg whites into the cream cheese mixture to lighten it.

- Carefully fold in the remaining egg whites in two batches, ensuring the batter maintains its airy consistency.

Baking:

- Pour the batter into the prepared springform pan. Tap the pan gently on the counter to release any large air bubbles.

- Place the springform pan into a larger baking pan. Create a water bath by adding hot water to the larger pan until it reaches about halfway up the sides of the springform pan.

- Bake in the preheated oven for approximately 1 hour and 20 minutes, or until the top is lightly golden and the cake is set with a slight jiggle in the center.

Cooling and Unmolding:

- Turn off the oven and leave the cake inside for about 10 minutes with the oven door slightly ajar. This gradual cooling helps prevent cracks.

- Remove the cake from the oven and water bath. Run a knife around the edges of the cake to loosen it from the pan. Allow the cake to cool completely in the pan on a wire rack.

Finishing Touches:

- Once fully cooled, carefully remove the sides of the springform pan. Dust the top of the cake with a delicate layer of confectioners' sugar.

Serving and Cloud-Like Bliss:

- As you relish each slice of the Japanese Cotton Cheesecake, experience the remarkable sensation of its cotton-soft texture. The airy lightness and subtle sweetness create a culinary symphony that melts in your mouth.

With the Japanese Cotton Cheesecake, you're embarking on a remarkable adventure that highlights the artistry of achieving a cloud-like cheesecake masterpiece. Each bite invites you to savor the delicate balance of flavors and textures, guiding you toward the captivating variations and inspirations that beckon your exploration.

Chapter 13: Mini Cheesecake Bites: Bite-Sized Bliss

Delight in bite-sized indulgence with Mini Cheesecake Bites, where petite portions of creamy cheesecake offer a symphony of flavors in each mouthful. In this chapter, we'll explore the art of crafting these delightful treats, perfect for sharing, gifting, or simply savoring the essence of Japanese cheesecake in miniature form.

Ingredients:

- 250g cream cheese, softened
- 50g unsalted butter
- 100ml whole milk
- 3 large eggs, separated
- 1/2 teaspoon vanilla extract
- 60g granulated sugar
- 30g cake flour
- 10g cornstarch
- 1/8 teaspoon salt
- Assorted toppings: fruit compotes, chocolate drizzle, nuts, berries, etc.

Instructions:

Preparation:

- Preheat your oven to 325°F (160°C). Line a mini muffin tin with paper liners.

Cream Cheese Mixture:

- Melt the cream cheese, butter, and milk in a heatproof bowl. Stir until smooth and allow the mixture to cool slightly.

- Whisk in the egg yolks and vanilla extract until fully combined.

Dry Ingredients for Mini Treats:

- Sift the cake flour, cornstarch, and salt together. Gradually fold the dry mixture into the cream cheese mixture until smooth.

Whipped Egg Whites:

- In a clean bowl, use an electric mixer to whip the egg whites until they become foamy.

- Gradually add the granulated sugar while continuing to whip.

- Whip the egg whites to soft peaks – they should be glossy and hold their shape.

Folding and Batter Assembly:

- Gently fold one-third of the whipped egg whites into the cream cheese mixture to lighten it.

- Carefully fold in the remaining egg whites in two batches, ensuring the batter maintains its airy consistency.

Mini Cheesecake Assembly:

- Spoon the batter into the prepared mini muffin tin, filling each cup nearly to the top.

Baking:

- Bake in the preheated oven for approximately 20-25 minutes, or until the tops are lightly golden and the cheesecakes are set.

Cooling and Topping:

- Remove the mini cheesecakes from the oven and allow them to cool in the muffin tin for a few minutes.

- Carefully transfer the mini cheesecakes to a wire rack to cool completely.

Assorted Toppings:

- Once cooled, adorn each mini cheesecake with your choice of toppings. Create a medley of flavors by adding fruit compotes, chocolate drizzles, chopped nuts, fresh berries, or any other delectable embellishments.

Savoring Each Petite Delight:

- With Mini Cheesecake Bites, you're entering a realm of delightful minis that encapsulate the essence of Japanese cheesecake in a compact form. Each bite-sized bliss offers a burst of flavor and texture, making them perfect for sharing moments of joy or indulging in a sweet treat.

Chapter 14: Tips for Perfect Baking and Texture

Achieving the perfect Japanese cheesecake requires a blend of precision, technique, and a touch of culinary finesse. In this chapter, we'll delve into essential tips and tricks that will guide you toward mastering the art of baking Japanese cheesecakes with a flawless texture.

Ingredients' Temperature: Ensure that your cream cheese, butter, eggs, and milk are at room temperature before starting. This promotes even mixing and prevents lumps in the batter.

Whipping Egg Whites: When whipping egg whites, use a clean, dry bowl and utensils. Any trace of grease can hinder the volume and stability of the egg whites. Adding a pinch of cream of tartar can aid in creating a stable meringue.

Folding Techniques: Gentle and deliberate folding of the whipped egg whites into the cream cheese mixture is crucial. Use a spatula and incorporate in a light, circular motion, ensuring you maintain the airy consistency.

Water Bath Technique: Placing your springform pan in a water bath (bain-marie) prevents the cheesecake from cracking and promotes even baking. Wrap the outside of the springform pan with aluminum foil to prevent water from seeping in.

Oven Temperature and Positioning: Preheat your oven accurately and maintain a consistent temperature throughout baking. Position your cheesecake in the center of the oven for even heat distribution.

Cooling Process: Gradually cool the cheesecake by turning off the oven and leaving the door ajar. This prevents drastic temperature changes that can cause cracks.

Parchment Paper Lining: Line the bottom of your pan with parchment paper to ensure easy removal without damaging the delicate cake.

Texture Variation: Adjust the texture by varying the amount of egg whites you fold into the batter. More egg whites result in a lighter, fluffier texture, while less egg whites yield a denser consistency.

Flavor Infusion: Experiment with different flavors by incorporating extracts, zests, or infusions. Subtle additions like matcha, citrus, or spices can elevate the taste profile.

Toppings and Garnishes: Elevate the visual appeal and taste by adding creative toppings. From fruit compotes to chocolate drizzles, toppings can enhance the overall experience.

Patience and Practice: Perfecting the art of Japanese cheesecake baking takes practice. Don't be discouraged by initial attempts – each effort brings you closer to mastering the technique.

Temperature Management: Store your finished cheesecake in the refrigerator to maintain its texture. Allow it to come to room temperature before serving to fully appreciate the flavors.

Chapter 15: Creative Toppings and Garnishes

Elevate your Japanese cheesecake creations to new heights by exploring a world of imaginative toppings and garnishes. In this chapter, we'll delve into a plethora of possibilities that will transform your cheesecakes into stunning culinary works of art, delighting both the eyes and the taste buds.

Fruit Medley Magic: Fresh, seasonal fruits such as berries, sliced kiwi, or passionfruit add vibrant colors and a burst of natural sweetness. Arrange them artistically on top or around the cheesecake for a visually appealing and flavorful touch.

Chocolate Drizzles: Create intricate patterns or simply drizzle melted chocolate over the cheesecake. Dark, milk, or white chocolate can add depth and contrast to the cake's appearance while enhancing its taste.

Caramel Elegance: A drizzle of luscious caramel sauce lends a touch of decadence and a rich, buttery flavor. Consider a caramel swirl on top or a pool of caramel sauce beneath each slice.

Whipped Cream Swirls: Dollops of freshly whipped cream provide a cloud-like contrast to the cheesecake's texture. Play with patterns, shapes, and flavors by adding a hint of vanilla, cocoa, or a splash of liqueur to the cream.

Nutty Crunch: Chopped nuts such as almonds, walnuts, or pistachios can add a delightful crunch and nutty flavor. Scatter them over the top or use them to create an artistic border.

Edible Flowers: Delicate, edible flowers like pansies, roses, or violets create an enchanting visual spectacle. These floral accents lend a touch of elegance and sophistication to your cheesecake presentation.

Candied Citrus Peel: Create your own candied citrus peel to adorn the cake. The vibrant colors and sweet-tart flavor provide a zesty contrast to the creamy cheesecake.

Fruit Compotes: Homemade fruit compotes, like raspberry or mango, add a layer of complexity and a burst of flavor. Serve alongside or drizzle over slices for a delectable pairing.

Shaved Chocolate and Cocoa Dust: Use a vegetable peeler to create delicate curls of chocolate that can be arranged in a stunning pile atop the cake. Dust the cheesecake with cocoa powder for a rustic yet elegant finish.

Flavorful Sauces: Infuse your cheesecake with extra flavor using sauces like berry coulis, passionfruit sauce, or even a touch of citrus-infused syrup.

Layered Creations: Opt for a layered effect by alternating slices of cheesecake with layers of fruit, cream, or sauces in a glass dessert dish. This visually appealing approach allows you to showcase a variety of textures and flavors.

Personalized Embellishments: Get creative with your own personalized touches, such as edible glitter, gold leaf, or even miniature meringues, for a unique and memorable presentation.

Chapter 16: Dairy-Free and Vegan Variations

Expand the joy of Japanese cheesecake to those with dietary preferences by exploring dairy-free and vegan variations that deliver the same delightful flavors and textures. In this chapter, we'll dive into innovative techniques and substitutions that allow you to create luscious dairy-free and vegan Japanese cheesecakes.

Ingredients for Dairy-Free and Vegan Cheesecake Base:

- 250g dairy-free cream cheese (e.g., cashew-based)
- 50g coconut oil (or dairy-free butter)
- 100ml coconut milk (full-fat)
- 6 tablespoons aquafaba (chickpea brine) or vegan egg replacer
- 1 teaspoon vanilla extract
- 120g granulated sugar
- 60g cake flour (or gluten-free flour)
- 20g cornstarch
- 1/4 teaspoon salt

Instructions:

1. Preparation: Preheat your oven to 325°F (160°C). Grease the bottom and sides of a 9-inch (23cm) round springform pan and line the bottom with parchment paper.

1. Dairy-Free Cream Cheese Mixture: Melt the dairy-free cream cheese and coconut oil in a heatproof bowl. Stir until smooth and allow the mixture to cool slightly. Whisk in the coconut milk and vanilla extract.

1. Vegan Egg Replacement: If using aquafaba, whip it with an electric mixer until stiff peaks form. If using a vegan egg replacer, prepare it according to package instructions.

1. Dry Ingredients for Dairy-Free Base: Sift the cake flour, cornstarch, and salt together. Gradually fold the dry mixture into the dairy-free cream cheese mixture until smooth.

1. Folding and Batter Assembly: Gently fold in the aquafaba or vegan egg replacer until fully incorporated, maintaining the airy consistency.

1. Baking and Cooling: Follow the baking and cooling instructions from previous chapters, adjusting the time if needed based on your oven and the specific ingredients used.

Chapter 17: Gluten-Free Options for Everyone

Embrace the diversity of palates by exploring gluten-free options that ensure everyone can enjoy the delightful world of Japanese cheesecakes. In this chapter, we'll delve into creative techniques and substitutions that allow you to craft delectable gluten-free Japanese cheesecakes that satisfy both taste and dietary preferences.

Gluten-Free Cheesecake Base:

- 250g gluten-free cream cheese
- 50g unsalted butter or dairy-free butter
- 100ml whole milk or dairy-free milk
- 6 large eggs, separated
- 1 teaspoon vanilla extract
- 120g granulated sugar
- 60g gluten-free flour blend (rice flour, potato starch, tapioca flour, etc.)
- 20g cornstarch
- 1/4 teaspoon salt

Instructions:

1. Preparation: Preheat your oven to 325°F (160°C). Grease the bottom and sides of a 9-inch (23cm) round springform pan and line the bottom with parchment paper.

1. Gluten-Free Cream Cheese Mixture: Melt the gluten-free cream cheese and butter in a heatproof bowl. Stir until smooth and allow the mixture to cool slightly. Whisk in the milk and vanilla extract.

1. Dry Ingredients for Gluten-Free Base: Sift the gluten-free flour blend, cornstarch, and salt together. Gradually fold the dry mixture into the cream cheese mixture until smooth.

1. Whipped Egg Whites: Follow the instructions for whipping egg whites from previous chapters.

1. Folding and Batter Assembly: Gently fold in the whipped egg whites until fully incorporated, maintaining the airy consistency.

1. Baking and Cooling: Follow the baking and cooling instructions from previous chapters, adjusting the time if needed based on your oven and the specific ingredients used.

Chapter 18: Fusion Flavors: East Meets West

Embark on a captivating culinary journey by infusing the enchanting world of Japanese cheesecakes with a fusion of East and West. In this chapter, we'll explore a realm of innovative combinations that bridge cultural influences, creating Japanese cheesecakes that harmoniously blend flavors from both hemispheres.

Matcha Mocha Swirl Cheesecake

Ingredients:

- 250g cream cheese, softened
- 50g unsalted butter
- 100ml whole milk
- 6 large eggs, separated
- 1 teaspoon vanilla extract
- 120g granulated sugar
- 60g cake flour
- 20g cornstarch
- 1/4 teaspoon salt
- 2 tablespoons matcha powder
- 2 tablespoons cocoa powder
- Espresso-infused chocolate drizzle (for topping)

Instructions:

1. Follow the instructions for the Cream Cheese Mixture, Whipped Egg Whites, Folding, Baking, and Cooling from previous chapters.

1. Divide and Flavor: Divide the batter into two equal portions. In one portion, fold in matcha powder until well incorporated. In the other portion, fold in cocoa powder.

1. Swirling Technique: Alternately spoon dollops of the matcha and cocoa batters into the prepared springform pan. Use a knife to gently swirl the batters to create a marbled effect.

1. Baking and Topping: Follow the baking instructions from previous chapters. Once cooled, drizzle a luscious espresso-infused chocolate over the top for a delightful fusion of flavors.

Sesame Cheesecake with Citrus Zest
Ingredients:

- 250g cream cheese, softened
- 50g unsalted butter
- 100ml whole milk
- 6 large eggs, separated
- 1 teaspoon vanilla extract
- 120g granulated sugar
- 60g cake flour
- 20g cornstarch
- 1/4 teaspoon salt
- 2 tablespoons black sesame paste
- Zest of 1 orange or tangerine
- Sesame seeds and orange segments (for garnish)

Instructions:

1. Follow the instructions for the Cream Cheese Mixture, Whipped Egg Whites, Folding, Baking, and Cooling from previous chapters.

1. Sesame and Citrus Fusion: Fold in black sesame paste and the zest of an orange or tangerine into the cream cheese mixture before incorporating the whipped egg whites.

1. Baking and Garnishing: Follow the baking instructions from previous chapters. Once cooled, sprinkle sesame seeds on top and garnish with orange segments for a delightful fusion of nutty and citrusy flavors.

Chapter 19: Charming Cheesecake Presentation

Elevate the experience of savoring Japanese cheesecakes by delving into the art of enchanting presentation. In this chapter, we'll explore creative ways to showcase your cheesecake creations, transforming them into captivating centerpieces that captivate the eyes and excite the taste buds.

Rustic Elegance with Fresh Berries:

Arrange an assortment of vibrant fresh berries, such as strawberries, blueberries, and raspberries, in an artful cascade over the top of the cheesecake. The natural colors and textures create an inviting rustic charm.

Whipped Cream and Chocolate Shavings:

Crown your cheesecake with a lavish layer of freshly whipped cream. Add a touch of luxury by generously scattering delicate chocolate shavings over the cream, creating an irresistible contrast of light and dark.

Edible Flower Garden:

Adorn the cheesecake with a selection of edible flowers, such as pansies, violets, or rose petals. Arrange them in an intricate pattern, allowing nature's beauty to take center stage.

Caramel Drizzled Artistry:

Drizzle a generous amount of rich caramel sauce over the top, allowing it to cascade down the sides. Create elegant swirls or patterns for a touch of indulgent drama.

Mosaic of Nutty Delights:

Embellish the cheesecake's surface with an assortment of chopped nuts, creating a mosaic of flavors and textures. Consider almonds, pecans, and hazelnuts for a crunchy masterpiece.

Elegant Minimalism with Powdered Sugar:

Embrace the beauty of simplicity by dusting the top of the cheesecake with a delicate layer of powdered sugar. This minimalist approach highlights the cake's elegance.

Chocolate Ganache Drapes:

Create a luxurious allure by draping the cheesecake with a velvety chocolate ganache. Allow the ganache to flow down the sides, adding depth and decadence.

Fruit Coulis Swirls:

Elevate your presentation by drizzling vibrant fruit coulis (fruit puree) in elegant swirls across the cheesecake's surface. The contrasting colors and flavors create an alluring visual effect.

Seasonal Sensations:

Embrace the flavors of the season by incorporating seasonal elements. For instance, delicate edible flowers in spring, fresh citrus slices in summer, or spiced apples in autumn.

Culinary Artistry with Gold Leaf:

Infuse opulence into your presentation by delicately placing edible gold leaf on select areas of the cheesecake. The glistening accents add a touch of culinary artistry.

Chapter 20: Exploring Japanese Cheesecake-Inspired Desserts

Venture beyond traditional Japanese cheesecakes and explore a world of delectable desserts that draw inspiration from their creamy, delicate flavors. In this chapter, we'll dive into imaginative creations that capture the essence of Japanese cheesecake while presenting it in new and exciting forms.

Japanese Cheesecake Parfait

Ingredients:

- Prepared Japanese cheesecake, cubed
- Whipped cream or coconut whipped cream
- Assorted berries (strawberries, blueberries, raspberries)
- Crushed graham crackers (gluten-free, if preferred)
- Honey or fruit coulis for drizzling

Instructions:

1. In elegant glasses or bowls, layer cubes of Japanese cheesecake with dollops of whipped cream, a sprinkle of crushed graham crackers, and a handful of mixed berries.

1. Repeat the layers, creating a visually appealing and decadent parfait.

1. Drizzle honey or fruit coulis over the top for added sweetness and flavor.

Japanese Cheesecake Ice Cream Sundae
   Ingredients:

- Prepared Japanese cheesecake, cubed
- Vanilla or matcha ice cream (dairy-free, if preferred)
- Toasted almond slivers or crushed nuts
- Matcha powder for dusting
- Chocolate syrup or ganache

Instructions:

1. Scoop a generous serving of vanilla or matcha ice cream into a bowl.

1. Top with cubed Japanese cheesecake pieces and a sprinkle of toasted almond slivers.

1. Dust the dessert with matcha powder for an extra touch of flavor and color.

1. Drizzle chocolate syrup or ganache over the top for a delightful contrast.

Japanese Cheesecake Stuffed Crepes
   Ingredients:

- Prepared Japanese cheesecake, sliced
- Crepes (regular or gluten-free)
- Sliced bananas or other fresh fruits
- Chopped nuts (walnuts, pecans)
- Whipped cream or coconut whipped cream

Instructions:

1. Lay a crepe flat and place slices of Japanese cheesecake along the center.

1. Add sliced bananas or other fresh fruits, followed by a sprinkle of chopped nuts.

1. Roll the crepe around the filling, creating a stuffed crepe.

1. Top with a dollop of whipped cream or coconut whipped cream and an additional sprinkle of nuts.

Japanese Cheesecake Truffles
Ingredients:

- Prepared Japanese cheesecake, crumbled
- Dark or white chocolate, melted (dairy-free, if preferred)
- Finely chopped nuts or cocoa powder for coating

Instructions:

1. In a bowl, mix crumbled Japanese cheesecake with melted chocolate until well combined.

1. Roll the mixture into bite-sized truffles.

1. Roll the truffles in finely chopped nuts or cocoa powder for a delightful outer coating.

1. Chill the truffles until the chocolate sets.

In this culinary voyage through the enchanting world of Japanese cheesecakes, you've embarked on a remarkable exploration of flavors, textures, and artistic presentations. From classic recipes that celebrate the delicate essence of Japanese cheesecakes to innovative variations that cater to diverse dietary preferences, you've woven a tapestry of culinary artistry that's both delightful and inspiring.

You've learned to master the intricate balance of ingredients, the art of whipping egg whites to ethereal perfection, and the secrets to achieving that sought-after cloud-like texture. Through chapters that unfold like a tantalizing menu, you've embraced the fusion of East and West, celebrated the beauty of presentation, and even ventured into a realm of delectable desserts inspired by the essence of Japanese cheesecakes.

As you savor each slice and share these delectable creations with loved ones, remember that you've not just mastered a recipe – you've cultivated a culinary journey filled with passion, creativity, and the joy of exploration. The pages of this cookbook are a testament to your dedication to the art of Japanese cheesecakes, and the possibilities you've unlocked are as boundless as your imagination.

So, whether you're indulging in the classic elegance of a Japanese Cotton Cheesecake, experimenting with fusion flavors that bridge cultural influences, or delighting in charming presentations that captivate the senses, your journey doesn't end here. It continues with each new creation, each inspired adaptation, and each imaginative twist that you infuse into your culinary endeavors.

Thank you for joining me on this delectable adventure through the Japanese cheesecake cookbook. May your kitchen be a canvas for countless culinary masterpieces, and may the joy of creating, sharing, and savoring continue to enrich your gastronomic experiences for years to come.

www.ingramcontent.com/pod-product-compliance
Lightning Source LLC
Chambersburg PA
CBHW021752150726
47989CB00004B/1627